Cambridge Marketing Handbook:
Philosophy

D1356575

Cambridge Marketing Handbook: Philosophy

A discussion on the philosophy of marketing

Charles Nixon

Publisher's note

Every possible effort has been made to ensure that the information contained in this book is accurate at the time of going to press, and the publishers and authors cannot accept responsibility for any errors or omissions, however caused. No responsibility for loss or damage occasioned to any person acting, or refraining from action, as a result of the material in this publication can be accepted by the editor, the publisher or any of the authors.

First published in Great Britain and the United States in 2013 by Kogan Page Limited in association with Cambridge Marketing Press.

120 Pentonville Road	1518 Walnut Street, Suite	4737/23 Ansari Road
London N1 9JN	1100	Daryaganj
United Kingdom	Philadelphia PA 19102	New Delhi 110002
	USA	India

www.koganpage.com

© 2013, Cambridge Marketing College.

The right of Cambridge Marketing College to be identified as the author of this work has been asserted by them in accordance with the Copyright, Designs and Patents Act 1988.

ISBN   978 0 7494 7071 5

British Library Cataloguing-in-Publication Data

A CIP record for this book is available from the British Library.

Design and layout by Cambridge Marketing College
Printed and bound by CPI/Antony Rowe, Chippenham, Wiltshire.

Dedication
To my wife and work colleagues from the past 30 years and to Peter Thompson who sparked my interest in marketing.

Biography

 Charles began his career after studying History and Economics at Manchester University, a degree that he says gives him a long term approach to strategy. He was first employed as Government Relations Officer for Courtaulds (then the largest textile company in the UK) where he liaised with civil servants and politicians on government policy. Whilst at Courtaulds he was asked to explore the possibilities of the use of new mini computers in the field of market research and intelligence. This led to his founding Courtaulds' Office of Market Intelligence for its Consumer Products Group and establishing one of the first computerised marketing information systems in the UK.

After a short spell at the International Wool Secretariat as Senior Economic Analyst, Charles went to Warwick Business School (WBS) to take one of its first MBAs. Whilst there he helped write the Business Plan for the Warwick Science Park and so confirmed his interest in High Technology. Following WBS he joined Arthur Andersen Management Consultants (now Accenture) and spent time in Chicago and Geneva, before joining Mercury Communications the then embryonic rival to BT. At Mercury, Charles was Head of Market Research and Market Planning helping the new company segment its market, plan for distribution, and research customer needs in order to introduce new products. In 1987 he moved to the City of London and joined Extel Financial in time for the Big Bang and the city revolution. These latter two posts gave Charles an insight in to the different ways UK companies approach the market and marketing.

It was during this time in London that Charles was asked to do guest lectures on Marketing in Cambridge, meeting Ian Brownlee with whom he was later to found the College.

Following several years with Extel he was head hunted by Societe General to rebrand its recently acquired UK Unit Trust Asset Management arm – Touché Remnant. However the lure of WBS proved too strong and in 1992 he left the City to start Doctoral Research on the Marketing of English Universities.

During this time Charles founded Cambridge Marketing College with, Ian in May of 1991. The College quickly established itself for its fresh and enthusiastic approach. Over the next five years it steadily grew as a part time activity and in 1997 expanded with a second college in Guildford and then a third in Manchester. In 1999, Charles became Chief Executive of the College. Since then, the College has gone from strength to strength to become the leading Professional Marketing College in Europe with 1,400 delegates at its 10 centres around the UK and from over 100 countries worldwide.

Contents

Conventions

For the sake of simplicity the following are interchangeable: He = She; Consumer = Customer = Business; Product = Service = Goods = Offering; Companies = Organisations

Word cloud produced through Wordle™ (www.wordle.net)

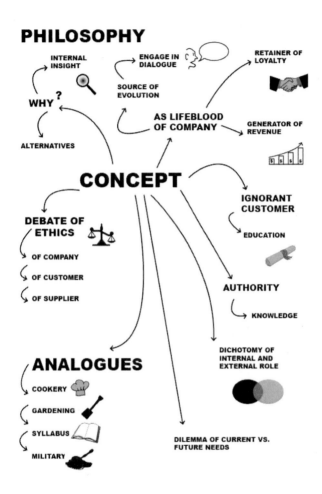

PHILOSOPHY

INTERNAL INSIGHT

ENGAGE IN DIALOGUE

RETAINER OF LOYALTY

SOURCE OF EVOLUTION

WHY?

ALTERNATIVES

AS LIFEBLOOD OF COMPANY

GENERATOR OF REVENUE

CONCEPT

IGNORANT CUSTOMER

EDUCATION

DEBATE OF ETHICS

OF COMPANY

OF CUSTOMER

OF SUPPLIER

AUTHORITY

KNOWLEDGE

DICHOTOMY OF INTERNAL AND EXTERNAL ROLE

ANALOGUES

COOKERY

GARDENING

SYLLABUS

MILITARY

DILEMMA OF CURRENT VS. FUTURE NEEDS

Infographic drawn by Lorna Brocklesby

Preface

I have spent 30 years marketing products and services for a variety of companies from textiles to high technology and financial services. I have worked in most aspects of marketing from research through strategy to implementation. For the last 20 years I have taught, consulted and advised on marketing for over 2,000 delegates of Cambridge Marketing Colleges. It is from this experience that I have developed the ideas in this Handbook and the guidance they offer.

Many books have been written on marketing; many on the individual elements of marketing; many on the sectorial applications but few, if any, are on the Philosophy of Marketing – Why do we need marketing? This Handbook aims to fill this gap and bring some perspective to our actions as Marketers.

The book is aimed primarily at those new to the subject, those unconvinced of the need for the discipline, and at practitioners who need to reflect on why they do what they do.

However, there is no case for "this does not apply to me"; marketing applies to all.

Acknowledgements

I would like thank all the staff and delegates of the College who have contributed to this Handbook. In particular, to Emma Garland for her patience and to Shane Minett and Kiran Kapur for their proof reading skills, which have been greatly tested. I would also like to thank Laurie Young for his advice and finally Malcolm McDonald for his insight and wisdom.

The Marketer's Poem:

An extract from:

We Are the Music-Makers
by Alfred O'Shaughnessy, 1874

We are the music-makers,
And we are the dreamers of dreams,
Wandering by lone sea-breakers,
And sitting by desolate streams;
World losers and world-forsakers,
On whom the pale moon gleams:
Yet we are the movers and shakers
Of the world for ever, it seems.

With wonderful deathless ditties
We build up the world's great cities,
And out of a fabulous story
We fashion an empire's glory:
One man with a dream, at pleasure,
Shall go forth and conquer a crown;
And three with a new song's measure
Can trample an empire down.

We, in the ages lying
In the buried past of the earth,
Built Nineveh with our sighing,
And Babel itself with our mirth;
And o'erthrew them with our prophesying
To the old of the new world's worth;
For each age is a dream that is dying,
Or one that is coming to birth.

Introduction

Whilst economics may be the underlying mechanism that drives the world it is surely the human condition that motivates it. Whether it be the desire to raise people out of poverty (however defined), to discover or acquire new things, or to improve quality of life by reducing hard labour, it is this driving urge that compels us as business men and women to work, to strive for new inventions and to constantly try to improve. Understanding this motivation is what lies at the heart of successful marketing.

How we use this understanding is the crucial act of our benevolence as marketers. As few consumers always understand their own motivations and actions, a great burden of responsibility is placed on us. We can exploit, protect or educate.

In this Handbook my aim is to set out ideas. It is for you to form your judgements. I do not use cases or examples that are quickly dated. My aim is to stimulate you to consider how an idea may apply to you.

What has marketing done for us? Well, it has brought about the state of the world we live in, and whilst we may complain (and in the UK we do) it has stimulated science, economics and communications. We now have healthier, longer lives, less need for the hard labour of our ancestors, a vast range of choice of material goods and services, and a global reach we never had before. The current generation of children will reach an average height of 6 foot and live to 90. Now I hear the cry "That's not marketing!" but read on and I think you will realise that without the successful competition that marketing engenders business would not be delivering these benefits.

A brief history of marketing
(An experienced marketer can skip this section)

A brief history of marketing evolution

Marketing has been around, though not known by that term, since commerce began. Logos of Roman merchants selling goods in the markets of Pompeii can still be seen.

To illustrate our history we can use a very simple analogy: that of bread. How many people buy bread on a daily basis? The majority of people would probably buy bread these days on a weekly basis, or perhaps twice a week. In the early days of the industrial revolution most people lived in a rural village and worked on the land and would have bought their bread on a daily basis. And because they lived in a small community, worked in that community, and shopped in that community, everybody knew where the baker was; he did not have to advertise, did not have to promote himself. In economic terms, they had perfect knowledge. In marketing terms, there was high customer intimacy.

If you travel today to some of the rural communities in Italy and Spain you will see exactly the same thing happening. You go on holiday, walk down the street and cannot find a baker's yet all the locals are walking past you with loaves of bread. You cannot find the baker's anywhere because there is not a big sign outside saying 'Bakery' or 'Patisserie'. It is possibly in someone's front room, yet all the locals know where it is and the baker does not need to promote himself.

However, as economies grew and industrialisation took place, people travelled from small rural village communities to much larger communities, or they moved into towns where they had no previous knowledge. Here they were not able to shop as regularly because of shift work. Goods also travelled further; the first canal was built in order to transport coal from the mines into Manchester. Railways were built not just to carry people, but mainly to carry goods. The result was that consumers did not have perfect knowledge of the market any more, and consequently producers had to communicate with these wider/larger market places. In addition, as the towns grew there was a requirement for multiple suppliers as one baker could no longer supply all needs.

To compete, our baker (who has moved from the village into Manchester) now has to **advertise**, to put boards out in front of his shop, to set a window display – basically to set out a 'stall' to say 'I am here'. These are mainly promotional tools, but other marketing tools are also being used. As a bright entrepreneur he says his market is changing its buying pattern.

Firstly, if you buy bread on a daily basis, you would consume it in a day and then go back and buy another loaf the following day. Therefore the manufacturer, the baker, only has to produce bread that keeps fresh for 24 hours. If you try and consume some traditional French or Spanish bread the day after you bought it, it is rock hard and is not particularly enjoyable. So with the changing shift patterns, the product in the industrial era now has to be **differentiated**. For those who are going to buy bread every other day it needs more moisture content so that it stays fresher for longer; for those buying on a weekly basis, the bread must have either preservatives in it or a wrapping to keep it fresher for longer. Thus some products are for the market buying on a weekly basis, and others for consumption on a more frequent basis.

Product division leads us to one of the strongest tools within the marketer's kitbag – **segmentation**. This concept divides or segments the market place into groups of customers (consumers) with similar desires e.g. people who want weekly bread, as opposed to people who want daily bread. The producer (the baker) can now price his product and distribute it differently. If it is weekly bread he can distribute it over a larger area because it stays fresh for longer. Further, the producer can assess the size of the different market places and produce enough of the right type of product to satisfy each market's needs. This allows the producer to identify which are the more profitable markets and therefore which to concentrate on. This is known as **targeting**.

As our baker progresses, he wants to grow and so takes advantage of the new transport technology – rail – and starts shipping bread to the next town. However, it does not sell as well as in his home town. Intrigued he travels to the new town one morning and observes the populous looking at his bread shop but going on to buy from a smaller local baker's. He asks why they are not buying. The answer? Because they do not know his bakery (although they have heard of a very good baker of the same name in the next town). Our baker reasons that he needs to educate the market that the two bakers are the same. To do this he needs to **brand** his products. And the best way to brand bread? On the bread! It is around this time (the mid-18th century onwards) that brands come into being as a means of communicating the quality of a product when it is sold far from its point of manufacture. The oldest product brand still in existence is Pears soap, dated from about 1789.

The growth of economic activity and marketing continued apace until we came to the Second World War. After the Second World War we had a period where within the UK we had a starved market place in terms of modern consumer goods. Technology and consumerism had continued apace in America, but the UK had rationing during the Second World War, as a result of which there was a tremendous latent demand. Rationing did not end until c.1951. We then went through a huge period of consumer boom. Consumers who had saved up disposable income were suddenly subjected to a barrage of new consumer products which offered them either convenience, speed, or some benefit to their modern life. Added to this there was a population boom and then the advent in the 1960s of mass communications.

A large number of companies were founded on the basis of mass communications. Marshall McLuhan made his famous statement that the medium actually is the message (McLuhan, 1964). The point he was making was that because a product was advertised on television it takes on a quality standard all of its own. This was true of the 1960s and 1970s with television and in the 1990s with the internet and now with social networks.

The good times went on very nicely until we hit a nasty recession at the beginning of the 1980s, and then hit another one at the end of the decade and the result of this was that marketing had to be re-aligned. Marketing people were in the habit of saying 'I need a marketing budget; I need to advertise; I need to do this and that promotion' and would get the finance on the basis that companies were growing fairly successfully and the result was that 'we must do advertising; it's been successful in the past'. Faced with a recession, the questions asked were 'Justify your expenditure. Why do I need to do marketing? What happens if I don't carry on marketing?' There was no answer. Marketing was in most instances unable to justify its spend because it could not show, as a salesman could, that 'I spent X thousand pounds either on salary or commission, and I brought in Y business'. There was no direct marketing correlation.

The result was a change in marketing. A combination of computer technology and a strain on advertising budgets gave rise to what we now call **Direct Marketing**. In the first instance this was in the form of direct mail, because it was extremely easy to justify. On the basis of a known number of letters sent out, if a response rate of X yields Y business we will reach the point where marginal costs equals marginal sales, which is a straightforward economic approach.

Another phenomenon also happens in a recession – a realisation that we cannot continue to lose customers if there are no new ones so we need to keep hold of existing customers. If it is assumed (and statistics vary) that it is more expensive to recruit a new customer than to retain an old one, the reaction may be 'Let's spend more money on building the relationship with our existing customers, rather than going out and trying to recruit new ones'. And so the concept of **Relationship Marketing** was born.

The twenty-first century has seen marketing evolve again and yet continue on the same path. The advent of the internet, the World Wide Web and Social Media has enabled marketers to get closer to their customers and now the emphasis is on engagement.

The development of digital communications (Email, SMS, MMS, and online advertising) has continued the trend of Direct Marketing, and the use of Social Media and Crowd Sourcing has added further dialogue mechanisms to our armoury.

Our history of marketing has taken us full circle from the pre-industrial situation where the baker knew his customers and matched his goods to their needs, to the contemporary idea of customer relationship marketing – which aims to do the same thing, only today we try to serve thousands if not millions of customers through technology.

However, one further aspect of the history of marketing also needs to be raised to understand the situation we find ourselves in today.

Marketing (in the UK) got off to a shaky start. In the early days of marketing as a business discipline (in the 1960s) many marketers in the UK felt there was a "God given" right to influence or even control the marketing mix. However, many marketing directors had little formal training and were often sideways appointments for managers from other areas.

The prospect of a gentleman (and it was a man) sticking his nose into the production area, sales territory, finance department or distribution section was (and often still is) seen as interference. As a result, barriers were erected and conflict ensued for those pursuing a marketing approach. The antagonism created in many companies spawned real problems for the growth of successful marketing in the UK.

Chapter 1: What is Marketing?
1.1 Some definitions

For many marketing is about communications and PR. It is the mouth piece of an organisation. It is also the eyes and ears – listening and observing the market place. So it should follow that marketing is also the "grey matter" in between these faculties – the brain driving an organisation.

Terminology has also confused the understanding of marketing. The term marketing is used imprecisely far too often. If as marketers we believe marketing is concerned with the wider realm of the marketing mix then we need to stop it being used as a surrogate for promotion. The result is confusion amongst the public and media as to what is meant when the word marketing is used. So here are some definitions:

> **Chartered Institute of Marketing**
> The management process responsible for identifying, anticipating and satisfying customer requirements profitably (CIM, 2009).

> **American Marketing Association**
> Marketing is the activity, set of institutions, and processes for creating, communicating, delivering, and exchanging offerings that have value for customers, clients, partners, and society at large (AMA, 2007).

However these definitions are inherently company centric and avoid the issues of the last two decades i.e. understanding the needs of individuals and society, and the environmental impact of production and waste. There is also the need to include the burgeoning issue of 'Well Being' i.e. the benefit of consumption or providing consumers with a better quality of life directly and indirectly. To this end a higher definition of Marketing is needed.

> **Higher definition of marketing**
> Understanding the needs of individuals and society as a whole and providing each with a better quality of life at an acceptable cost.

1.2 The evolution of attitude

If we accept the higher definition the next question is when does it apply. Companies evolve through many stages as they grow and at each stage marketing plays a part.

Orientation is a technical term used in academia to indicate a company's mind-set or attitude to business. The classic discussion has been about various stages of orientation as a progression with market orientation seen as the nirvana of a company's mental evolution.

Figure 1.1 The evolution of orientation – part I

However, the premise that the orientation flows in a one-directional way is flawed. Having been in businesses for several decades, I have often observed that companies go through several iterations of these orientations with market orientation continually having to battle to regain pre-eminence. In reality it is a cycle that companies have to manage and balance as they grow.

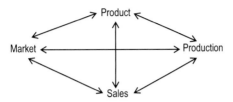

Figure 1.2 The evolution of orientation – part II

I would also take issue with the term marketing orientation. I have seen too many companies get swept into the arms of the 'marketing men'. By this I mean a belief that customers are 'punters' with little intelligence and that they can be 'marketed to' in order to increase corporate sales/profit often determined by the short term needs of shareholders. The cynicism that pervades these companies allows them to oversell products that can be faulty or indeed dangerous.

This is really the concept of selling via marketing techniques. In highly competitive markets, intense marketing is inevitable to preserve market share or to sustain a viable company. But the degree to which appeal is based on the lowest common denominator (often price) eventually removes the value from the market, leaving only those suppliers with the cheapest means of production and a consumer who buys on price and believes the product to be a commodity. I therefore do not adhere to this orientation.

There is no set cycle or order to a company's change of orientation but it goes something like this. At start-up a company is **Product Orientated**. It is fixated on the need to get its offering right and to solve the problem it has identified in the market. At this stage, potential consumers may not even realise that they have a problem which needs a solution. Entrepreneurs often say that customers do not know what they want and that is why the classic marketing approach does not always work for start-ups.

Having convinced enough customers to buy, the company then needs to sell its product into the market before competition grows too strong and here **Sales Orientation** is adopted. Then to meet demand and/or deliver cash flow for NPD (New Product Development), companies classically become **Production Orientated** – going down the learning curve as quickly as possible.

It is at this point that companies are meant to evolve into **Market Orientation**. Many do as they become empathetic with customers and evolve to meet their needs. However, it is not as simple as that as companies have to continue to generate cash in order to maintain their existing corporate structure. So usually sales orientation is still needed as is production orientation. In addition, as the company develops new offerings it may also become product orientated in order to innovate. The balancing of these competing mind-sets is what 'politics' in companies is often about.

It is often said that companies that do not constantly change or evolve their offering, die (consider Jack Welch's famous comment that "If the rate of change on the outside exceeds the rate of change on the inside, the end is near.") and it is true that customers are often looking for innovation in order to excite them into purchasing. In addition new technologies bring new possibilities. And for that reason, companies need to be skilled at spotting or developing new markets. Market orientation is critical for the long term survival of companies but it needs to be balanced with the need to maintain the existing business.

To achieve this balance many companies hive off the marketing culture to a separate division in order to nurture it and avoid clashing with the other orientations. In other instances development work is hidden (the IBM skunk works that produced the original PC being an example).

It is possible to argue that true market orientation only exists in the pre-start-up phase of a business where a need has been identified and a solution is being developed without the constraint of supporting the on-going survival of other aspects of the business.

To trade successfully companies need a variety of skills in their management structure. I am often told at courses I teach that "I wish my boss was here to hear this, then they would understand what we need to do." My reply often comes as a surprise. "Do you know what your boss does and what their problems are?" Running a business is not easy and is often a balancing act between competing parties. Too many marketers remain ignorant of the competing issues in running a business. As practitioners of a discipline which claims insight into all aspects of the market, marketers need to have a general understanding of the other business skills – especially finance.

Observational research is often the best way to inform a business. If possible be your own customer. If not then observe and talk to them on a daily basis. The modern predilection for Social Media is a drive to connect and 'have a dialogue' with customers by some companies that otherwise sit in 'Ivory Towers' and 'Silos' and carry out the functions assigned to them by scientific management (Drucker, 1994) rather than actually having conversations with their customers (who should be their friends and not only via Facebook). The customer is not always right, but then neither is the company so a discussion is needed to educate both as to what is possible and practical.

Having travelled a fair deal in my early life and then for business it has often occurred to me that travel broadens not only the mind but it enlivens the soul, informs the intellect and inspires the entrepreneur. Go further and prosper should be the motto of the young budding entrepreneur in the 21st century.

1.3 The Marketing Mix

No discussion of Marketing would be complete without a word about the Marketing Mix. Put simply the Marketing Mix is the set of tools which can be coordinated by marketers to meet customers' needs. The term was first coined by Neil Borden, Emeritus Professor of Marketing and Advertising at the Harvard Business School (Borden, 1948) but has evolved over the decades. Initially there were 4 elements known as the 4Ps:

1. **Product (or service)** – that is offered by the company or organisation.

2. **Price** – the charge for the use/consumption of the Product.

3. **Promotion** – the communication of the offering to the market via advertising, PR etc.

4. **Place** – this is how the products get to market or the consumer (This is also known as Distribution but "3Ps and a D" is not so memorable!).

As services began to dominate the economy 3 more elements were added to the mix:

5. **People** – the human interface that assists enquirers to gain information and then to assist in purchase. Also to further assist in the optimum usage of the product/service.

6. **Process** – the mechanism by which customers enquire and then purchase.

7. **Physical Evidence (or Packaging)** – the manner in which a service is made tangible or a product is wrapped.

To do justice to the wider scope of stakeholder marketing we need to go still further and adopt the Nicklin 10Ps and add:

8. **Political Power** – and regulatory control.

9. **Public Opinion** – including social media.

10. **Partners** – and Stakeholders.

By adopting this simple check list a company, institution or individual can consider how best to vary the elements in the Mix to gain better sales, adherence to an idea or increase popularity.

A note on branding

The brand is perhaps the single most important concept to be invented by marketing. It raises the mere product-offering to the iconic. By adding values and emotion, branding gives companies the power to engage with customers on a psychological level. Like the naming of characters in a novel much hangs on the sound (notably the vowels) and this plus the iconography can create powerful loyalty (or ridicule). However, branding has to be done carefully.

With this loyalty also comes responsibility for the quality and ethics of what is on offer. The trend for brand extensions as the safest method of product development can increase influence over people's lives or weaken the brand to the point where no one understands what it stands for. As marketers we are the "movers and shakers" and we must preserve the integrity of what we offer if the customer is to evolve with us. Devalued, discarded and hollowed out brands litter the history of business and with it the growing cynicism of the public.

Chapter 2: The Spectrum of Marketing
2.1 What does marketing do?

In the context of our higher definition of marketing you will not be surprised that the role of Marketing also needs a fresh take. In this modern era the role of marketing in an organisation needs to be recognised as far broader than just meeting customers' needs. It must include:

Marketing as an aid to planning

As you will appreciate, day-to-day business activity takes precedence. So, when it comes to thinking about the future and what the company might do that it does not currently do, then marketing provides the tools.

Companies live within the market and need to understand how it is evolving. As practitioners of audit techniques for macro and micro external environmental analysis such as PESTER and the 5 Forces, marketers need to become experts in understanding the environment in all its incarnations. This knowledge should lead to unrivalled insight into the market, customer and competition. From this comes **Authority**.

Within a company, finance departments have power and exercise authority because they understand the 'numbers'. Production has authority because they understand the mechanics of creation. Marketing, in order to be a meaningful part of the company, needs authority and this must come from knowledge of the market.

Marketing as a champion of the customer

This goes beyond acting as the champion of a market oriented approach within the company. Marketers need to represent the wider issues of society and to act as the social conscience of a company. They need to align the demands of all an organisation's stakeholders (including its customers) with the wider needs of society and the environment in which it operates. Enterprises sit in the environment and must be part of it. In part this is about Social Marketing i.e. using marketing to achieve behavioural change for the good of society. But it also means that marketers should stand up for the good of the customer within a company. If a new product is proposed that might benefit the company but not be good for the consumer it is the responsibility of marketers to say so. Supersize what?? Indeed, is this not what customers expect (even pay a premium for) when they invest money and faith in a brand. It is all about **Trust**.

Marketing in economic exchange

Figure 2.1 shows the exchange process of information, communication and products that is needed to bring about successful transactions. This is perhaps the purest form of marketing. With constant contact with the customer, the flexibility inherent in SMEs brings the elements of the marketing mix into high relief. Their ability to adapt the product offering, price, distribution and service to individual customers brings about an empathy often unsurpassed by big business until the latter diversify in order to evolve.

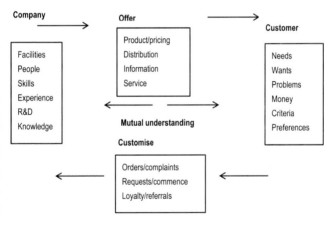

Figure 2.1 The exchange process

Marketing as a stimulator of innovation and creativity

Now this fits neatly with the marketers' mantra of giving the customer what they want. And indeed in broad terms all companies must meet the wants of their consumers. However the marketer must add to the basic want of the market in order to achieve the goal of growth and a better world. If we respond to the blinkered demands of the market then we end up responding to the lowest common denominator e.g. TV ratings or junk food which does not take into account the good of the consumer. As in the quote attributed to Henry Ford when asked about market research "If I'd asked my customers what they wanted, they would have said a faster horse."

The point here is that the marketer knows what it is possible to create from the technology the company has developed. They have knowledge the consumer does not have and are therefore able to envisage new products and services not merely the extension of existing ones.

This means it is incumbent on marketers to innovate. Taking the earlier criticism about over consumption of basic products, it must be our mantra as marketers to offer the new, the better, the next level. As such we are the movers and shakers in the ode and the bringers of the new world.

Marketing as a leveller

The role of marketers in driving innovation can be taken a step further. Marketing is a great leveller and divider. It creates new/improved products and services and strives to make them available to all that can afford them. And for those that cannot it innovates until they can.

2.2 Where does marketing apply?

The reaction to marketing can range from enthusiastic adoption to "it doesn't apply to me". The latter tends to come from individuals and organisations that do not see commerce as their prime aim and are more concerned with the quality of the products or services they offer.

Historically these have been artistic and charitable organisations, though over the last 20 years, the latter have embraced what has been called Social Marketing, in which the tools of marketing have been used to change citizens attitudes and actions, for example to end drink driving. In general, however, in today's world marketing applies to everything you want it to. As a set of tools and discipline of thought it can apply to churches, schools, charities, health services, companies and individuals who have some thing/idea/message/or character they wish to sell. Some talk about the brand of the individual: I am my own brand!

Chapter 3: The Philosophy of Marketing
3.1 Why do we need marketing?
Is there a reason for marketing?

Does it add to the body of business knowledge? The honest answer is 'No'. Sociology and psychology tell us about how people behave; economics tells us how markets react and mathematics provides the basis for financial management.

Like all social science disciplines it is not essential or naturally formed. It is a convenient set of models to assist in the age old task of creating a successful company. And by "successful" I mean one that achieves its aims, even if those are only survival or subsistence for the employees. However, marketing does bring all of these disciplines together and provides a unique focus on the marketplace and the customer.

Do we need marketing?

The answer lies in the fact that all other business disciplines are functional whether finance, production or human resources. Marketing is philosophical. In short it is about the customer, how they behave and why organisations need to understand them.

Surely the true test of a word is to see if there are other words to replace it in most contexts. If there are then there is no need for it.

So what are we doing when we are marketing?

1. We are promoting our goods, advertising or communicating
2. We are researching the market for customer reactions or consumer needs
3. We are developing or launching new offerings

Is there anything we are doing when we are marketing that is not something else?

Probably not.

Is the term therefore only a convenience?

No, as it embodies more than a set of actions. It embodies a way of thinking about the economic (and social) intercourse of companies and individuals. Marketing is a process, a methodology and a philosophical approach to business that transcends the purely financial and transactional. In its fullest incarnation it can even be counter to short term profit maximising (the primary goal of many economic theorists and investors).

In many organisations marketing was originally seen as a distinct department which was mainly responsible for the communications activity of a company. In answer to a visitor's question 'Where is marketing?', a receptionist might answer 'Down the corridor on the left'. Today, in a market-orientated company, as we have already seen, marketing must permeate all aspects of the business, and so the receptionist's response in a modern company might well be 'All around you'. There are still elements of marketing, especially research and communications, that require specialists but for market-orientated companies, much of the marketing idea is understood by all or most of the staff. Marketing is the driving philosophy of the business.

3.2 What characterises good marketing?

Marketing means different things to different people so firstly we need to look briefly at how marketing is viewed in different sectors before we can establish a set of guidelines for its use.

Are consumers the puppets of multinational corporations as in "No Logo" (Klein, 1999) or are they intelligent decision makers actively engaging with corporations for mutual benefit. Is the customer king?

One way to come to a conclusion is to look at how marketers (in a company) describe their other halves (those they are having the relationship with): Targets – very militaristic; Potential – exploitative. In modern terminology many would call them Stakeholders or Partners.

Let us start with the most virulent of these – marketing as exploiter. An exploiter of people, their ignorance and time. The overselling or miss-selling of products and more latterly services has often been based on exploitation of customer ignorance. One advertising adage states that all products can be sold on the basis of fear or greed. Add to that sex and you can account for 90% of advertising. Unrestrained promotion has raised many fears and concerns over pollution, obesity, the impact on children and health, and has resulted in controls on the marketing of financial services, drugs, food and health issues amongst others.

Yet there are two counter arguments. In order to have an effect, advertising must be accepted and acted upon by consumers. So does the consumer have a role? Secondly, in order to educate people about issues, legislators use the same marketing and advertising techniques to change social attitudes and habits: Get fit, stop smoking etc. During the 1990s the UK Government instigated the greatest increase in what is called "Social Marketing" ever seen in order to get policy messages across. You cannot travel the country these days without being told to do (or not to do) some of the most basic things. The Government was trying to achieve its policy objectives using marketing.

This leads to an interesting dilemma. Junk mail (and advertising) is greatly disliked. However, information and knowledge about new ideas and products is welcomed. Indeed whole television programmes are dedicated to it (and I don't mean the shopping channels). This leads to: marketing as informer and educator. The consumer is keen to know more but is often only sold to, not informed. The customer is king but kept in ignorance.

When marketers are seeking to exploit they look mainly to the quick sale and, like the stock market and some bankers, are only interested in the short term. They will resort to short selling in the financial world (selling something they do not have) and selling on price in the marketing world. Little thought is given to the long term consequences – it is all about achieving targets.

However, when a different approach is taken and marketers seek to educate the customer, a different relationship becomes possible – treating customers as partners. Initially many companies inform and educate their customers in order to promote their products but taking the next step and treating customers as partners develops a two-way relationship, with customers providing their comments and criticisms so that the company can improve its offering. Taken in today's context this means engaging in crowd surfing as a way to develop new products and social media to encourage dialogue with your customers.

Partner

Companies recognise the value of a two-way relationship. Customers' ideas and feedback are valued and used to improve and develop new offerings

↑

Educator

Companies recognised that customers do not always know what they want or what is technically feasible. Marketing was used to inform.

↑

Exploiter

Companies used marketing to sell as much of their product as possible. Communications were outward facing. Understanding of customers was used to increase sales.

Figure 3.1 The progression of marketing

Chapter 4: Consumer Dialectic

The classic dialectic is now between the conservationist, ethical consumer and the innovative, technical marketer.

The ethical consumer says:

"I have needs but do not want to harm the planet."

"I wish to live a very good quality of life but not through the exploitation of others."

"I am happy to pay a fair price."

"I wish to be able to conveniently purchase many goods but not be over supplied."

"I do not want waste."

"I have a lot and others have little – this is wrong."

The marketer responds:

"I can supply your needs but there is a cost to be paid in terms of the resources used."

"You demand 'goods' at a price that is competitive. This impacts on the costs we can pay suppliers which impacts on the prices/wages they pay."

"Your lifestyle is busy so you want convenience. This you pay for but predicting demand is not easy and some oversupply will occur."

"We agree with the disparity but is it our responsibility to get it right?"

Further the marketer says:
"Not all customers are the same, some buy the most convenient, others the cheapest, there are always more different tastes and needs to be met. There are 7.1 billion of us and growing at about 90,000 a day."

"There are also many competitors who have to find ways of differentiating offerings."

But the customer says:
"You supply too many options. Life is complicated enough but to shop these days is a battle too. Too many varieties, too many brands, and so much waste!"

"I don't get what I want. I get what you want to supply. And you are trying to trick me by not telling me everything. You use words to hide meaning and don't make things clear."

"Yes, you should put the world to rights if you caused the problem. Look at what happens when you make us eat too much."

The marketer responds:
"We only exist to serve your needs. It is the tenet of our creed that the Customer is King. We only supply what is demanded and if you do not buy then we cease to supply."

"There is some oversupply because of the changing balance of supply and demand which cannot be helped."

"Do you want to restrict supply to just a few options? The last time that occurred it was called communism and look where that led."

"Who is to select which options are to be supplied – Government?"

"We may have supplied the goods but you were the one who ate too much. Is that our fault? Surely you must bear most of the blame?"

"Besides you often don't know what you want. We have to try new things to see what you will buy. Not all work."

The debate can (and does) go on but the axes are drawn:

Information	V.	Ignorance
Consumption	V.	Waste
Exploitation	V.	Relationship

The overall issue is one of **Trust**. Marketers serve two masters: internally the management and stockholders of the company and externally the customer. How well that balance is maintained produces the **Ethics** of the company.

Companies and their marketers are guilty of over-marketing. They can over stimulate demand by 'psychological marketing' – appealing to the fear and greed instincts of consumers, they play tricks of 'Brand' juggling – retiring and recycling brands to stimulate the marketplace, as they conceal information about products.

On the other hand, the consumer is not a passive participant and in many cases actively engages in the process through greed or ignorance that can be easily overcome.

The role therefore, for marketers is to **educate, inform and stimulate**.

The other side of marketing is **Creation**. The essential part of the waves of Creative Destruction (Schumpeter, 1947) that are crucial to the evolution of the economic society.

Consumers do not always get what they demand because they do not always know what they want – they do not know what is possible. No one asked for a mobile phone. Yet R&D is constantly creating possibility out of technology. For all the wastage and inefficiencies we have the advanced world of today because marketing introduced these new ideas to society and some of them were accepted.

In the modern market economy the consumer has never had it so good. Yet if companies are only responding to the demand of the market then by extension the consumer is to blame for sweat shops, exploited resources and poor wages. Yet no consumer actively seeks these things. From the consumers' point of view it is the 'Marketing Men' who are to blame. "Trying to sell me stuff I don't need resulting in waste; obesity; child exploitation; over consumption. They did not tell me about the implications of my purchases".

Thus one of the impacts of business and marketing over time has been a build-up of ignorance. There is then, of course, the argument that if they (the company) do not take care of us (the customers) then the state should do it. However, a result of this has been what some call the nationalisation of family or the nanny state.

So it behoves consumers to think about the implications of their purchases and to take an active role and for marketers the imperative has to be for education of consumers.

4.1 The role of the ethical consumer
Are consumers interested in the impact of their consumption? Yes, of course they are. However, the question should really be how much are they interested? How far will they go to reduce the impact of their consumption? And how confusing is it to consume responsibly? Organic products are good for the environment. But what if they are flown in from Africa? Is this an environmental or charitable purchase? Once again the answer lies, at least in part, in information. A fully informed consumer is able to make better choices.

The customer is, as a consumer of multiple products on multiple occasions, an equal partner in the marketing process. Gone are the days when the consumer was ignorant of marketing methods and could be sold to with the old tricks of the trade. Today many are savvy from a very early age. Decry this fact or not but today's children understand advertising and marketing and it is a valid and accepted (by most) part of 21st century economic life.

Let us take this further then and put some responsibility on the consumer. It is no longer a free ride. There are obligations on the consumer to reduce the environmental impact of marketing.

With the rise of instant communication consumers can enquire and request information, leaflets, brochures, catalogues etc. at a whim. But most do not purchase. The company is then faced with the dilemma of whether or not to continue to pursue the potential customer – which costs both time and resources.

The consumer must shoulder some of the responsibility. Whilst legislation requires companies to offer opt-out boxes, should it not also be standard practice for customers to tell companies when they are no longer interested in their goods or services?

More subtly the option should be for a one-off interest in a good/service or a continuous interest. The benefits from cost saving and environmental reduction are obvious.

The answer once again is to educate, not control, and to do so honestly.

4.2 The role of the ethical marketer

Marketers are often driven by the short term demands of corporate stakeholders and engage in constant re-segmentation and fragmentation of the market in order to create new sub categories where none often exist to start with. The number of varieties of fruit juice and washing powder are good examples of the proliferation of products that results.

On the one hand this constant barrage of new brands (and recycling of old ones) may seem a waste of resources however it does yield the most effective mechanism of stimulating the ability to innovate rather than allowing the continuation of stagnant offerings. Marketing assists if not facilitates the waves of creative destruction that change our society.

The "mental affliction of prosperity", "addicted to money" – these and other phrases attempt to summarise the problems that unregulated

Marketing has produced. As a nation we are addicted to buying things. Those opposed to marketing believe there is a higher plane that we as a society should aspire to: an intellectual level that is not about consumption but about ethereal thought and development of the human condition and that, as we have satisfied all the basic layers of Maslow's Hierarchy (Maslow, 1943), we as marketers should be pushing citizens to heights of self actualisation.

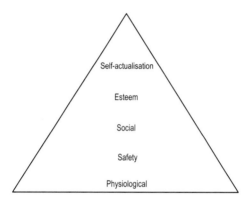

Figure 4.1 Maslow's hierarchy of needs

However, the bulk of existence is taken up with satisfying the basic levels of need, the constant reinforcement of their satisfaction and the striving to make that satisfaction more perfect.

Since commerce began, the need to feed, clothe and provide shelter has driven the bulk of demand. Given our advanced society should these needs diminish or are they constant? The over consumption of these goods comes from ignorance and not over selling. For the consumer, like an addict, it is easier to do more of the same when told it will bring the same level of satisfaction each time, than it is to stop and seek something different.

In the same way that some employers now feel the need to train new recruits because the state education system has not equipped them with essential skills, then so must marketers educate their customers. Life is not all about asset accumulation and shopping for things we do not really need. Marketing should not be based on a desperation to sell things but should come back to the fundamentals and help people achieve a better life.

4.3 The marketer's dilemmas
i) Promoting on the basis of price alone is immoral!

Do you feel angry or stressed when shopping? Do you feel that you are being "sold at" or offered goods that you do not need? Do you worry that the earth's resources are being turned into goods which are then wasted?

The latest 3 for 2 or Buy One, Get One Free (BOGOF) offers that appear to be a "bargain" are often nothing of the sort. The intention to consume all of the items eventually, does not always materialise. How many times have you bought one of these offers and ended up throwing at least some of the unneeded extra away?

Do you wonder how much you are really saving when you purchase a special offer? Do you stop and consider what the true cost of the product is – where it was made and by whom?

Gradually we have seen more evidence of goods reflecting the demands for a more ethical approach to production. A slow process – too slow for some. The problem often lies with companies that have gone through the market orientation phase and now need to maintain their growth by selling more (irrespective of whether there is any further demand).

The use of words

What are we doing when we say 'saving'? The word 'saving' brings on an irrational desire to purchase – not everything but those items we would like to have or believe we will eventually use. 'Was £9.99 now £5.99' brings the idea that it is a bargain, that it might not be that price always and therefore…

As marketers we are aiming to ensure purchase to increase sales and hopefully profit. And through this we secure jobs for production workers and industry staff. From the corporate perspective we are doing our job. From the purchasers' perspective we offer the ability to buy what they want for less or at an affordable price. Philosophically the question is 'do we do harm by this policy?'
Firstly, if we lie about the saving i.e. the higher previous price was not actually one that the product was ever sold for, then we are breaking the law. But if the higher price was genuine but only for the minimum legal period required, then we are being immoral.

Why is it cheaper to buy "9 branded toilet rolls plus 3 free" for less than the price of 12 own label recycled ones? The obvious answer is the margin the supplier is happy to make. But a better question (and one that is being asked more often) is "How much profit is justified? And at what cost to the planet's resources?" Many, including The Economist, would argue that competition and the profit motive is the most efficient regulator of development. Others would argue that solitary pursuit of profit is damaging lives and the planet.

The balance between these two arguments is still very uneven primarily because most people enjoy the levels of consumption the system brings without being overly concerned with the social cost. However, as the degree of concern grows and evolves to embrace wider aspects of the way we live, how does business need to respond? Are we doing harm with our pricing, are we encouraging over-eating or waste?

The counter argument is that if we do not make these offers then our competitors will, and they will be more profitable and faster growing. This is sound but only if those are the only recognised goals.

Long term survival of a company is dependent on its reputation and steady performance. Forget the few behemoth corporations that occupy the headlines – the long term successful company is the one with loyal trusting customers who believe in what the company says and does.

So if you suffer from unscrupulous competitive pricing, then educate your customers as to why you do not follow suit. Profit is not the only motive for long term success.

ii) Doing damage

The Business of Business is Business. This famous phrase widely attributed to Milton Friedman is often quoted to dismiss the idea of corporations doing good works expressly. Yet we are all part of society so we should not harm it by our actions. How can a marketer continue to promote products that are causing harm?

Firstly let us consider if the product harms by itself. Many recent examples fail to give good weight to the fact that the customer is a part of the equation and is unlikely to be ignorant of the 'down-side' of purchase or over consumption. In these instances, information and education must be the duty of the marketer. The marketer's role is to inform and educate not to encourage wanton consumption of unneeded goods.

Is it wrong for a chocolate maker to offer sports equipment in return for loyalty to the brand? Cadbury's introduced a points scheme for sports equipment with each purchase. They were criticised by pressure groups for encouraging over-eating. However, not everyone is going to over indulge in chocolate, and given that the product is not on the warning lists for medical reasons, it seems perfectly acceptable to offer support for another activity that its customers enjoy.

In America, what the National Rifle Association's (NRA) argument states is that it is not guns that kill; it is people who kill (it is not chocolate or burgers that make people fat; it is eating too many of them). Consumers do the eating but marketers are complicit in the harm that is done.

We must consider the welfare of our customers not just that of our shareholders!

The marketer has an internal and an external duty. It is a competitive market and a campaign that gains sales over rivals is the essence of the marketer. The internal duty is to secure the cash flow to maintain the existence of the company. Externally it is to look after the welfare of its customers and on this axis it might be possible to level a charge. However, even here the engagement of the customer would be better.

One of the aspects that the Cadbury's example highlights is the changing nature of attitudes in society. Three factors are at play here:

- The role and the rabidity of the press (always critical)
- The abdication of customer responsibility (decline of caveat emptor)
- The image of enterprise/businesses as exploitative, especially by the media

This status quo can move marketers to have greater direct contact with customers. Through social media and crowd sourcing marketers are now able to engage directly with prospects and customers. This allows marketers to educate and inform the market directly. However, it will also have implications for the responsibility companies will have to take if they do not use social media to inform.

iii) The internal dilemma
Traditionally there has been much conflict between departments over the exercise of the marketing mix: with R&D and production jealously guarding their right to develop new products, finance often controlling the pricing debate and, the most common, with sales over access to customers.

It is this latter area that needs to concern us most. The lack of access to customers is an issue for many marketers. If we are not able to meet, talk to, and observe the market place we lose our authority.

For others marketing is seen as a cost centre and sales as the revenue earner. I believe it is our imprecise definition of marketing that has led to much of the problem. In many companies marketing means communications and promotion and as such is not seen as strategic or involved in planning.

This is one of the fundamental dilemmas of our discipline. The skills we claim and the authority we can wield makes us fundamental to the development of any company. Yet the way we have allowed ourselves to be defined corrals us into a technical function. It is interesting to observe that in new digital/internet companies there is often no such dilemma. Communications is one function and marketing is another.

iv) The final dilemma – who does marketing?

At the tactical level it is not just marketers! Increasingly, marketing is out evolving itself. A wide range of workers in companies carry out marketing functions, though often they are not called marketers and may not have been educated about the role. Yet understanding and relating to customers is what delivery drivers, receptionists, customer service staff and sales people do.

For many of the Generation Y, marketing is a natural part of life. As a young child they recognise when they are being sold to and can deconstruct an advert by their early teens. They see commercial life as part of the environment and as such are comfortable with it and understand much of what goes into it. Most of the generation in their 20s and 30s who work in marketing have little formal training as their implicit experience is sufficient to help them do the day to day tactical tasks. However companies are often letting them play with commercial weapons that they do not understand. Hence the constant use of large blunderbuss sales campaigns which fail to achieve their ROI.

The dilemma is too much experience versus too little knowledge.

On the other hand at the strategic level marketing is much too important to be left to marketers! Here the debate about marketing directors on the board abounds.

For many, the power of strategic marketing is left in the hands of too junior a staff. Knowledge is essential, but execution is critical to a successful marketing strategy and therefore the best exponents of the art are those with the experience and knowledge to implement and these are rare in too many companies.

There is one further sobering thought: that the discipline and theories of marketing have now passed into common understanding. So like the typing pool of the last century which has disappeared because we are all typists now; so marketing as a function is out evolving itself and we are all marketers now.

Chapter 5: How to View Marketing

I present these as alternative ways of seeing the marketing process. Choose one that matches your outlook. If you do not "get "one of them then it is not for you:

- As gardening to grow a successful business
- As a curriculum to use all types of knowledge
- As cookery to create business
- As war to engage in conflict
- As chemistry to assemble the right elements

5.1 Marketing as gardening

Gardening is a very useful analogy for many companies as it not only presupposes 'seasons' (which exist in most markets) but also recognises that successful gardens take several years to come to fruition. Gardening also has the element of 'hardy' plants that will "over winter", not die in adverse climates and come back in full vigour next year.

The planning and layout of a garden are crucial. You will see gardeners arranging plants in a new bed much further apart than you might want them but this is to allow for growth, and requires a good image in the 'mind's eye' as to what the result in terms of shape and colour will look like. This requires patience as well as skills and experience which in turn require time to accrue. These attributes are not always something that is easily available today as instant results are often demanded.

The choice of plants is critical to achieving the desired garden and we also need to prepare the ground, add nutrients and water. These raise interesting questions about what they might be in the marketing world. Further, we also need plenty of sunlight and we have no control over this macro environmental factor. All of these we may liken to the marketing mix.

Strong plants never emerge if you keep disturbing the roots. Don't keep innovating just for the sake of it.

Pruning is also essential in a garden to obtain and maintain the design and shape you want.

Plants are also prone to diseases and constant breeding is needed to develop resistance. And then there are the competitors – the weeds which need constant attention. You may take the analogy further.

A good book using this analogy was Planting Flowers, Pulling Weeds by Rubio and Laughlin (Rubio and Laughlin, 2002) which considered the issues of growing profitable customers.

5.2 Marketing as a curriculum
This is an interesting analogy as it shows how fundamental marketing is to life.

Maths	Assessment of profitability
Economics	Understanding the market exchange
English Literature	Inbound communications
English Language	Outbound communications
Geography	Understanding the location and delivery aspects of the market
Biology/Psychology	Understanding the customer make–up
Chemistry	Understanding interactions in the market
Physics	Understanding the mechanics of technology
Sociology	The groupings of the market
History	Building relationships
Languages	International marketing
Religion/Philosophy	Understanding customer beliefs and motivation
Art	Branding and design
Physical education	Concern for health and well-being of customers

5.3 Marketing as cookery

"The recipe for success" is an old and popular phrase for all sorts of arenas. And it fits marketing well. The mix of ingredients is well known (the 7Ps) but is constantly added to with new 'spices or seasonings' (the 10Ps etc.). However, like cookery the secret is in blending the ingredients.

The nice thing about this analogy is that certain standard recipes do work time and time again. And this is often sufficient to maintain sustenance for the corporate body. It is when we try to achieve more (build the body, grow or go faster) that imagination and new recipes are required.

New 'superfoods' in marketing come around regularly – social media is the latest ingredient needed in everything and may well become a standard part of the marketer's pantry.

Similarly new techniques come along to speed up the process or reduce the manual effort – automated mailings or mobile marketing.

One of the important parts of the analogy is planning. When a chef cooks, the process starts well before entering the kitchen. The objective is assessed – a dinner party, a family meal, a BBQ? Who is coming? Family, friends, business, etc. What do they like? Indeed in today's society the rise of catering for special dietary needs mirrors the fragmentation/segmentation of markets.

So the chef assesses the required outcome, the customer base and their needs, and then plans the courses (as a campaign). At that stage the ingredients are assembled so that the plan can be executed. This aspect is worth reflecting on because many marketing campaigns drift or tail off after they first burst. Sometimes this is because the necessary follow up items are not in place. Meals are very rarely abandoned between courses.

Also think of the structure of dinner parties. They start with an appetiser to whet the taste buds, and are then added to in layers (courses or dishes) which give a variety of flavours that complement one another. Having satisfied the palate, we need to revive the guests and so coffee and chocolate (known stimulants) are served at the end.

Finally, (though this analogy could fill a book) there is the important aspect of marrying wine with food – perhaps best seen as sales and marketing.

5.4 Marketing as war

The military metaphor is everywhere. The terminology that business people tend to use is based on the original ideas of warfare – strategy, tactics, campaigns, targets, etc. even books on offensive marketing (Davidson, 1987).

It is a natural analogy given the derivation of the term Strategy (from strategia meaning generalship), but nevertheless forgets an important element. One of the greatest writers on war, Carl von Clausewitz said in 1832 that "War is merely the continuation of policy by other means" (Von Clausewitz, 1993). Is the analogy therefore that marketing is merely the pursuit of business by another means?

5.5 Marketing as chemistry (or alchemy)

The simple analogy here is that elements are combined to create materials suitable for a specific purpose. The interesting aspect about this analogy is that it is scientific and therefore implies a certain exactness which marketing lacks.

Marketing is often referred to as an art not a science as the outcomes are not predictable. Whilst this is true in the detail it is not at the macro level – so a degree of science should be considered as part of the discipline. As such, let us explore the analogy of chemistry a little more:

Similarities:

- Need to have the right elements
- Need to practise to be able to predict outcomes
- Importance of equipment and preparation
- Need for a controlled environment
- Need to be able to repeat experiments
- Need for precision

The lack of control over the environment outside a laboratory would seem to eliminate the analogy. Nevertheless there are discussions about the need to do more controlled testing of business policies in order to predict the outcome. The rise of the so called 'Big Data' does perhaps give us the opportunity to monitor and thereby better understand the impact of campaigns.

Chapter 6: The Six Spheres of Marketing

Taking analogies a little further, we can take the idea of spheres of activity. Aristotle had 52, Ptolemy had 26. We as marketers operate within six spheres:

1. Psychological – understanding the individual and their personality; how they were formed by nature and nurture; how they retain information and process it; their needs and wants; their motivations and reactions.

The driving force of most markets is the motivation of the individual. The complex nature of the decision making process and the innumerable variations of the factors influencing the purchase maker make this a fascinating subject and it is lamented that more of the behavioural side of marketing is not taught.

Personal influences on the consumer include:

- Genetics
- Self-perception
- Memory
- Learning (non-formal)
- Experience
- Attention
- Motivation
- Age

2. Sociological – upbringing; education and family; social groupings; (tribes!); peers; cultural background; ethnic influences.

As individuals we may live alone. As consumers we interact with others and so marketers need to understand what impact this has on decision making and the enjoyment of products.

We often believe we come to our own decisions (except in B2B) yet we are always receiving stimuli from those around us:

- Ethnicity
- Family
- Peers
- Group norms
- Social grouping
- Reference points including opinion formers and leaders
- Education

Gladwell has written convincingly of the point at which products go from niche players through to mass market: The Tipping Point (Gladwell, 2002), and much of this is via social networks and business groups and that needs to be recognised.

Even in the situation of B2B marketing we are still dealing with human beings. They still inhabit the same social world and, although they may be more rational and objective in their decision making, they are still influenced by social pressure.

This point about humanity is very important. For all of the talk of internet marketing and social media, the customer remains a human being who lives (most) of their time offline.

Social media adds a very interesting dynamic to the sociological aspect of marketing, in that the groups that influence people are no longer limited by physical proximity and therefore many of the social and psychological barriers to forming such groups are broken down. The implication for marketing is that having found a market online the issue of satisfying it can become significant as it may be anywhere in the world. Consequently, distribution becomes a major part of the mix for any new online company.

Finally, a word on education. As I have already argued it is incumbent on the marketer to take a role in the education of his market. The constant debates over the quality of education systems in different countries aside, no customer has all of the knowledge base that the supplier has. Neither do they have the same mind set in terms of outlook, norms, or standards, and it is important to the long term relationship that the company and the customer are on the same wave length, speak the same language, have the same aims. Therefore, education via information and training is essential for each customer. Further, for the customer this adds to the experience of the brand.

3. Economic – how we derive value; how we afford; how we allocate our scarce economic resources.

The driving imperative behind marketing is mainly the economic exchange of goods and services. The rise of 'Not for Profit' marketing or social marketing adds additional motivation but economics is still clearly essential for the ongoing survival of such an organisation. Therefore we need to understand fully the mechanics of economic exchange and the elements that influence consumers:

- Cost of living (inflation)
- Cost of doing business (interest rate/exchange rate)
- Level of economic activity (employment rate/new building)
- Level of confidence
- Level of funds (household debt or business debt)
- Purchasing patterns

The exchange process is simple (see Figure 2.1 in Chapter 2) and involves the offering (supply) being demanded and consumed. However, the difficulty comes in matching needs and the offering in terms of product and in terms of level.

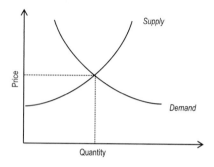

Figure 6.1 Supply and demand

The essence of marketing here comes back to understanding the customers' needs and the customer knowing what is on offer.

4. Polity – the sphere of political influence; controls and sanctions; local, national and global issues and organisations.

As the world grows more tightly connected and the World Wide Web allows rival groups to become more powerful, Government becomes concerned about corporate power over their citizens. The World Trade Organisation, G20, etc. act to ensure fair and free trade. The UN, EC and other multi-state groups act to maintain a balance of power. All of these impact and constrain marketing activity as they act to protect their citizens from exploitation and seek to control the unbridled flow of trade that might cause damage. Marketing needs to monitor:

- International regulation
- National regulation
- The bias of political parties
- Changing balance of agendas of those in/out of power
- Local politics
- Legislative programmes
- The control over personal freedoms

5. Technological – the impact of new technology; communications; and information management.

This sphere is often the most attractive to marketers because it deals with newness and innovation. Marketers are often looked to embrace new technologies quicker than other functions in order to exploit the competitive/commercial advantages it might bring.

- New products (digitisation)
- New communication technology (social media)
- New delivery technology (apps)
- New opportunities (genetics)
- New threats (genetics)
- New means of payment (M-Pesa)

This constant watching brief is a very powerful element in the armoury of marketing. Constant environmental scanning and hypothesising about the outcomes has spawned a new term and industry – Thought Leadership (Young, 2013).

6. Ecological – how we affect the environment.

The growth of the planet's population to 7+ billion and its likely increase to 10 billion in 2050 leads many to have concern about the impact this will have on the sustainable use of resources. Whilst the economics of recession may be more to the fore in consumers' minds at the moment, there is no doubt that many now have an ethical/ecological element to their consumption. Marketers need to ensure they consider the growth of this aspect as a factor in consumer and business behaviour.

- Carbon footprint
- Reuse – recycle
- Biodegradability
- Energy, water and raw material usage
- Method of production
- Packaging

From the above, a 'Periodic Table' summarising the main elements of marketing can be created.

Cambridge Marketing Handbook: Philosophy by Charles Nixon

PERIODIC TABLE OF MARKETING ELEMENTS

Planning	Mix elements and Isotopes		Communication mix	Market places	Customer	Stakeholders	Metrics
Audit	Product	NPD. Portfolio	Advertising	B2C	Psychological elements	Customers	Enquiries
Internal	Price	Elasticity	PR	B2G	Learning	Suppliers	Conversion %
External macro	Place	Direct indirect	Sales promotion	B2G	Memory	Media	Sales
External micro	Promotion	Media Message	Direct Sales	G2C - Social	Ego	Owners	Loyalty
Competition	People	Skills	Direct Media	NFP	Attitude	Impacted Public	Advocacy
Market	Process	Service quality	WOM	P2P	Motives	Employees	Reputation
Objectives	Physical aspects	Design	Exhibitions		Sociological elements		Share of voice
STP	Political		Sponsorship		Social groups		Understanding
Mission	Public opinion		Thought leadership		Peers		Awareness
Values	Partners	Affiliates	Digital isotopes	Research	Family		
Direction	Brand	Product v corporate	Social media	Secondary sources	Religion		
Mix plans			Mobile media	Primary sources	Culture		
Budget			Email	Sampling	Ethnicity		
Implementation			Www	Questioning			
Control			Blog	Observation			
			Curation	Analysis			
			SEO	Crowd Sourcing			

Conclusion

Marketers live in the world and are a fundamental part of that world. As such we have responsibilities. Marketing is also an accepted part of life. It is not to be apologised for. With the demise of any accepted alternative model of economic life (communism) the success of the social market economy incorporates marketing at its heart if not its soul.

References

AMA (2007) [online], *Definition of Marketing*,
http://www.marketingpower.com/aboutama/pages/definitionofmarketing.aspx
(Accessed 25/06/2013)

Borden, N H (1948) The Concept of the Marketing Mix, *Journal of Advertising Research,*
Classics, Volume II, September 1984

CIM (2009) *Marketing and the 7Ps A brief summary of marketing and how it works*, [online],
http://www.cim.co.uk/files/7ps.pdf (Accessed 25/06/2013)

Davidson, H (1987) *Offensive Marketing: Or, How to Make Your Competitors Followers*,
Penguin Books Ltd, 2nd Revised Edition

Drucker, P F (1994) *The Practice of Management*, Butterworth-Heinemann Ltd

Gladwell, M (2002) *The Tipping Point: How Little Things Can Make a Big Difference*,
Abacus, New Edition

Klein, N (1999) *No Logo: Taking Aim at the Brand Bullies*, Picador

Maslow, A H (1943) A Theory of Human Motivation, *Psychological Review, 50*(4), p370–96

McLuhan, M (1964) *Understanding Media*, Routledge & Kegan Paul

Rubio, J and Laughlin, P (2002) *Planting Flowers, Pulling Weeds: Identifying Your Most
Profitable Customers to Ensure a Lifetime of Growth*, Wiley

Schumpeter, J A (1947) *Capitalism, Socialism and Democracy* (Second Edition), 2010
Reprint, Martino Fine Books

Von Clausewitz, C (1993) *On War*, (New Edition), Chapter 3, Everyman

Young, L (2013) *Thought Leadership: Prompting Businesses to Think and Learn*, Kogan
Page

Index

This Philosophy Handbook is one in a series of Handbooks for marketing practitioners and students, designed to cover the full spectrum of the Marketing Mix. The other Handbooks include:

1. Product
2. Pricing Points
3. Distribution
4. Communications
5. Services
6. Research
7. Stakeholder
8. Law
9. Digital